Body Psychology: The New Body Language - Utilize & Understand The Power of Nonverbal Communication

Aiden MCcoy

© 2015

Disclaimer

Table of Contents

Introduction

Chapter 1: So What *Exactly* is Body Language?

Chapter 2: Why Body Language Matters

Chapter 3: Reading the Body Language of Others

Chapter 4: Refining Your Own Body Language

Chapter 5: Tips & Troubleshooting

Chapter 6: The Benefits of Understanding Body Language

Conclusion

Introduction

Effective communication is not all verbal. Our posture, facial expressions, eye movements, and gestures—our *body language*—speak just as loudly as our words. In fact, they often reveal more about our true thoughts, feelings, and intentions than we wish to convey. You know that feeling that the person you're speaking to isn't saying what they really mean? It's usually the result of a disagreement between verbal language and body language. If we are not paying attention, our body language can outright contradict our words, seriously compromising the power of our speech.

In developing an understanding of body language, we empower ourselves to communicate more effectively. In aligning our own body language with our words, we convey a clearer message and we leave a stronger, more lasting impression. In learning to interpret the body language of others, we give ourselves reliable insight into their true thoughts and feelings. We can even use body language to project confidence and authority when we do not actually feel them, enabling ourselves to turn moments of doubt into moments of success.

To understand body language is to understand people, and understanding is the foundation of trust. Most successful people do not work alone. They tend to be very influential leaders, and it is trust that persuades others to believe in their ideas and support their efforts. An understanding of body language, then, is one of our most powerful tools for achieving our goals and manifesting our dreams.

This book will provide you with more than a technical understanding of non-verbal communication. It will teach you to interpret the body language of others, giving you insight into their real needs and desires and enabling you to build trusting relationships. It will also teach you to use body language to support your own verbal expressions, enabling you to communicate clearly and leave a lasting impact that will inspire devotion from friends, family, and others who can assist you in accomplishing your goals.

You will also learn how not to use body language and how to avoid misinterpreting signals from others.

Chapter 1: So What *Exactly* is Body Language?

Body language is non-verbal action that outwardly reflects thoughts, feelings, needs, and desires. It includes everything from our tone of voice to the way we walk. For example, muscle tension, skin coloring, and rate of speech are all indicators of our stress level. Movements of the limbs, torso, and eyes tell us whether or not someone is interested in what we have to say. Breathing rate, perspiration, and vocal pitch illustrate our confidence or lack of it.

The movement of a single part of the body can carry as much meaning and as many different connotations as any individual word. We use our teeth, our hips, our hair, and our elbows to convey our thoughts and feelings to others. The tongue, for example, can project as many different emotions while silent as it can by helping to form words. We can convey a childish petulance and cheekiness by sticking our tongue out at someone. Licking the lips can indicate lust for a person or hunger for food, or it may reveal stress, which is often signified by a dry mouth. A person may also bite their tongue in order to keep from saying something offensive.

Just like in any other language, the individual words of body language can be combined to form sentences and entire stories. Individual elements of non-verbal communication often come in *clusters* that reveal more about a person's thoughts and feelings than a single action could. When interpreted in combination, a person's tone of voice, eye movements, and heart rate create a more complete and accurate picture than their heart rate alone. For example, a person's heart rate may speed up significantly due to extreme fear *or* extreme happiness. By interpreting their posture and eye movement as well, we discover which one is the case.

There are certain clusters of body language signals we all recognize. Take aggression for example. If a person were to stare straight into your eyes and hold your gaze while lowering their body into a wider, more stable stance and clenching their fists, they would not have to tell you they wanted to fight. You would know based on your interpretation of their body language. The cluster of body language that exhibits relaxation is also familiar to most people. It consists of even breathing, smooth, open gestures, and a gently attentive gaze. Clusters of body language elements can depict dominance, boredom, submission, and trust. They can be used to make sales, enhance romance, or deliberately deceive an observer.

While body language differs across cultures and individuals, there are certain *Core Patterns* that most people instinctively employ, whether they are conscious of it or not. For example, the *closing* pattern is commonly used to deny, refuse, or defend. Its elements include crossed arms, a lowered head and chin, and closed mouth and eyes. The opposite of that would be the *expanding* pattern, in which we thrust the chin and chest outward, lift the head, and spread the arms and hands in order to make ourselves appear bigger and more powerful. Other common and easily recognizable patterns include *protecting, flirting,* and *offering.*

It is important to remember that no element of non-verbal communication is performed in a vacuum. As acting teachers like to tell their students, *action is reaction.* A person's body language is triggered by external events and the words and actions of others. This means that the significance of an act of non-verbal communication can vary depending on the situation. Your co-worker may cross his arms as a means of defense, or to illustrate his feelings of superiority.

Because body language is always the result of a cause and effect scenario, interpretation can be complicated. That is why experts have broken the process down into five elements. A *cue* is the external event or internal thought that triggers a person's emotions, to which they react with body language. So, when your colleague crosses his arms, ask yourself, *what just happened that may have triggered that gesture,* or *what might he be thinking?*

The next element to look for is the *change*. If your colleague suddenly uncrosses his arms and assumes a more open position, search the previous moments for events that may have inspired that change. Perhaps the focus of the business meeting shifted from his accidental accounting mistakes to another employee's theft of $10 million, relieving the pressure on him and allowing him to drop his defenses.

When interpreting body language, the real challenge lies in deciphering *clusters*. As mentioned above, clusters are groups of non-verbal communication signals. These may occur all at once or in succession. When every movement in a body language cluster indicates that same thing, interpretation is easy, but if two or more actions contradict one another, they send a mixed message. Perhaps your colleague has uncrossed his arms and leaned back into an open, relaxed sitting position, but his face has reddened and his breathing has quickened. Contradictory physical signals from another may cause you discomfort. If so, ask yourself why you're uncomfortable.

Character also plays an important role in the significance of body language. Familiarity with a subject's personality allows you to interpret their body language with more accuracy. If you know that your colleague is an introvert, you won't mistake his limited, precise movements with timidity. Because personality makes such a big difference in the body language a person uses, it is important to avoid filtering another person's behaviors through the tinted lens of your own personality.

Perhaps the most important factor to consider when interpreting body language is *context.* Your colleague may be thinking about and reacting to aspects of his personal life at the same time he is reacting to the environment of the business meeting. Perhaps while the boss was praising him for a job well done, his wife sent him a text accusing him of infidelity. Even if he were actually a very humble man, it would be easy to assume that his crossed arms indicate a feeling of superiority brought on by his boss's praise.

Changes in body language may not always be obvious and concrete. In addition to clearly visible changes, body language can also consist of extremely small, subtle, and fleeting movements. Experts refer to these as *micro-expressions*. Lasting between $1/25^{th}$ and $1/15^{th}$ of a second, they typically betray emotions a person is trying to hide. Micro-expressions typically take the form of barely perceptible twitches of the eyes, mouth, or hands. They often play a major role in the interrogations of suspected criminals, but we all use them for various reasons. If you feel uncomfortable with someone and cannot explain why, you could be unconsciously registering negative micro-expressions.

Another very revealing form of non-verbal communication is an individual's effort to maintain what is commonly called the *comfort zone.* Social norms dictate the appropriate distance between two people depending on the circumstances. In regulating our proximity to others, we send a variety of differing messages. We use distance to demonstrate affection, to keep ourselves safe, to threaten others, and to make communication easier or more difficult.

E.T. Hall, in his book *The Hidden Dimension,* named four distinct zones of socially acceptable distance. The first is the *public zone,* which applies to situations in which we are surrounded by strangers. People usually maintain a distance of about 12 feet in the public zone. In the *social zone,* it is socially acceptable to shorten that distance to as little as four feet. The social zone allows us to maintain a safe and comfortable distance while connecting with people we may not know well. The *personal zone,* which shrinks the socially acceptable distance to as little as 1.5 feet, facilitates direct, focused conversation between two people who are interested in one another. The *intimate zone* is relatively self-explanatory.

These zones vary according to culture, personality, circumstances, and social background. A person who grew up in Manhattan may be more accustomed to being physically close to strangers, while a person who grew up on a farm in North Dakota may find closeness to strangers uncomfortable. People from heavily-populated Asian countries may lean in or move close to converse with someone they don't know well, while an American from Nevada will keep his distance. Likewise, someone who lives alone in their own suburban house will maintain greater distances than someone who lives on a commune, sharing every space and everything with everyone else who lives there.

Body language is complex and it is driven by many factors. It can be subtle or overt, and it can either reveal the truth or hide it. Developing an understanding of how to interpret it and how to use it will enable you to improve all of your relationships and accomplish your goals with greater ease.

Chapter 2: Why Body Language Matters

The ability to persuade others is essential to success in every aspect of life. No matter what our goals are, it is more than likely that we will have to work with others at some point in order to achieve them. Whether your goal is to start a business or to start a family, you will need to persuade someone else, or maybe many others, to support your endeavors, and studies have shown that body language is a highly effective tool for persuasion.

Every human being is conditioned by their upbringing and life experience to regard certain behaviors as cues. For example, a child brought up with an abusive alcoholic parent would learn to associate the smell of beer with physical violence. As an adult, this person would automatically feel afraid and physically threatened whenever she smelled alcohol.

In the same way, conditioning enables us to predict the actions of others based on body language. If a boy's mother always brushed her hair back over her shoulder before hugging him, he may interpret this behavior as a sign of affection. Conditioning leads to positive and negative reactions, and as people get to know one another, they learn what body language elicits happiness, sadness, comfort, or anxiety in a particular individual.

The ability to read another person's body language and to understand their reactions to your body language enables you to use non-verbal communication to gain their trust, affection, and devotion. Let's return to the woman raised by the abusive alcoholic father. As an adult, she meets a very perceptive man who learns her life story and adjusts his body language to make her feel safe, protected, and loved. She will likely return his feelings of affection, and they will be able to build a long-term loving relationship.

Studies also show that our own body language affects how we feel about a person, an idea, an event, or a situation.

According to research by Brinol, Petty and Wagner, published in *The European Journal of Social Psychology*, when a person is reading a message, straight, upright posture makes them feel more confident about the information than slouched posture. Research from Tom, Pettersen, Lau, Burton, and Cook, published in *Basic and Applied Social Psychology,* agreed with those findings, concluding that people preferred the same object more if the person offering it to them was nodding rather than shaking their head. Yet another paper by Strack, Martin, and Stepper, published in the *Journal of Personality and Social Psychology,* concluded that a person's enjoyment of cartoons increased if they were smiling.

This means that your ability to persuade a person lies in your ability to convince them to change their body language. People are happier, more receptive, and more confident about the subject at hand if their posture reflects happiness, openness, and confidence. If the person you want to persuade is sitting down, their arms and legs crossed, get them to stand up and go for a walk with you.

The change in posture will alter their perspective and their feelings about your proposal, whatever it may be.

They key to obtaining someone else's help and support is to encourage them to trust you. You can do so by altering your body language to project confidence, and by pitching your proposal to them while they are using confident body language themselves.

Overall, the power of body language lies in the fact that it changes our feelings about our situation. Altering our own body language can shift our own feelings as well as the feelings of others. This means that our ability to influence others and to gain their trust and support relies on our understanding of non-verbal communication. An ability to read and employ body language is one of our most valuable tools for achieving success.

Chapter 3: Reading the Body Language of Others

We begin conversations with others long before we first open our mouths to speak, and even if our words are critically important to our listeners, it is our non-verbal first impressions that will determine whether or not those listeners hear, understand, and value them.

Think about the last time you watched someone give a speech. Were they engaging and interesting? Did you have confidence in their expertise? Did you want to hear more, or were you waiting for the speech to end? Your answers to these questions will depend on the various elements of the speaker's first impression. Did they stride onto the stage, stand up straight at the podium, smile, and make eye contact with their audience? Or did they shuffle nervously into the room, fiddle awkwardly with the mic, and look down at their notes as they began to speak?

A confident first impression commands the attention of an audience and lends authority to a speaker's assertions, persuading listeners to adopt his or her point of view. The non-verbal expression of confidence consists of five basic elements: posture, eye contact, gestures, speech, and tone of voice. The speaker stands up straight with his or her shoulders back. Eye contact is solid and accompanied by an inviting smile. The speaker's hand and arm gestures are smooth, purposeful, and deliberate. Speech is clear and slow, the tone of voice low to moderate.

Effective communication is challenging even when we know that our audience is interested in what we have to say and that they are likely to agree with us, or at least appreciate our insight on the subject at hand. But expressing ourselves becomes even more difficult in situations that demand persuasiveness.

Think of an instance in which you had to pitch an idea to someone and convince them that they should support your efforts to bring it to fruition. Maybe you were interviewing for a job. Maybe you were requesting financing for an expensive project. Maybe you were negotiating a contract, a price, or a deadline. We all find ourselves in situations like these, and it is rarely the case that the person to whom we are speaking is patient and receptive, willing to listen carefully and come to a full understanding of our proposal before rejecting it. On the contrary, the other person is typically defensive and determined to have his or her way.

There are five ways to tell if you are talking to a brick wall. As before, they include gestures, facial expressions, posture, eye contact, and tone of voice. These are the five basic elements of body language, and they will reveal the thought process and feelings of any person in any situation. In a case of defensiveness, you would notice minimal facial expressions, very little eye contact, and gestures that keep the hands and arms close to the body. For example, your listener may cross his or her arms in front of their chest, gaze around the room or determinedly down at their knees, and either deliberately or subconsciously avoid reacting facially to anything you say.

They do not want to give you the impression that your ideas are affecting them.

Defensive body language invites confrontation, which is not productive not matter what the situation. If you perceive defensiveness in the body language of your listener, you can alter your language or your approach in order to make them more comfortable and more receptive to your ideas. Likewise, if you find that you are feeling defensive, you can avoid confrontation and facilitate productive conversation by altering your body language to reflect confidence.

Exhibiting confident, open-minded body language is as advantageous when addressing groups as it is when addressing individuals. Whether we like it or not, many of us find ourselves either working within, managing, or presenting to groups of people. Perhaps, as a member of the group, you are trying to be heard above a din of strong opinions. Or, as a supervisor, it may be your responsibility to delegate tasks to each individual in a group and ensure that their efforts coalesce to produce a solid, well-rounded solution to one specific problem. As a speaker, you may need to attract and maintain the attention of a group of people with varying areas of interest. In either case, the right body language can help you command the undivided focus of every person in a group and ensure that they listen to, fully understand, and most importantly, believe and agree with what you have to say.

Being alert to the signals of disengagement will help you adjust your words, actions, and tone of voice in order to make every person in the room feel that you are speaking directly and exclusively to them. Signs of disengagement include slumped posture, glazed eyes, and distracted hand movements such as scribbling, tapping, or fiddling with hair and clothes. If a member of your audience exhibits these behaviors, make eye contact with them and talk about their specific role in the project at hand. For example, if you notice your graphic arts expert drifting off, engage her by facing her, looking her in the eye, smiling, and asking for input on logo design.

Giving others the impression that you are listening to them is just as important as making sure they are listening to you. After all, you must give respect in order to receive it. One great way to show respect for your listeners is to use body language to demonstrate your appreciation for their time, their energy, and their thoughts on your presentation. If a listener asks you a question, take a moment to formulate a carefully considered answer. In doing so, you tell your listener that their question was insightful and valuable. There are certain body language signals that illustrate reflection and contemplation, such as stroking your chin with your fingers, or tilting your head, looking away, and re-engaging with your questioner once you have an answer.

Remember, body language is not a one-size-fits-all concept. Ideally, we would spend time studying people we wished to read and interpret, but there isn't always time for that. Therefore, it is important to keep in mind that different personalities use non-verbal signals for different reasons. An introvert may exhibit signals commonly associated with timidity, but that doesn't necessarily mean they *are* timid. They just have a different style of expression.

Also, there is a good chance that the person you're trying to read has some knowledge of the effects of body language. It's especially important to take this onto consideration when you're trying to gauge someone's truthfulness. For example, if your subject knows that most people break eye contact while lying, he or she may deliberately *over*-use it in order to avoid arousing suspicion.

Even when the person you are reading is sending obvious non-verbal signals, it is wise to take a moment to ask yourself what their intentions might be. For example, if someone is comfortable being physically close to you, they obviously like you. The question is, do they like you romantically, as a friend, or in a familial way? Looking at the context of your relationship with that person and at their other relationships will help you interpret their signals more accurately. If he or she is already involved in a romantic relationship in which they seem happy, their affection for you is likely more friendly in nature. They may also be the kind of person who feels very comfortable being physically close to *everyone* they like or love, in which case, maybe their feelings for you are similar to their feelings for their siblings.

Context is always important. Every non-verbal signal varies in meaning according to the situation. Take the lowered head for example. This can be a sign of shyness or an indication that someone is hiding something, or the person may just be taking a moment to consider the last thing you said. Culture is a very important aspect of context. In some cultures, lowering one's head is a way of showing respect. Likewise, some cultures embrace larger gestures and louder vocal tones while others prefer more reserve.

In general, an ability to read the body language of others will improve interactions and relationships of all types. Just make sure that you always consider personality differences, cultural differences, and the context of the other person's actions. This may seem like a lot to think about, but don't worry: with enough practice, paying attention to body language and the factors that influence it will become second nature.

Chapter 4: Refining Your Own Body Language

In working to refine your non-verbal communication skills, you come closer to gaining the trust, confidence, and support of those with the power and resources to help you achieve your goals. There are several ways in which you can alter your body language in order to elicit certain responses from people, and they can be used in a variety of situations.

Virginia Satir, an American social worker and family therapist, discovered through her work that certain stances are capable of revealing the emotions of a speaker *and* of causing the listener to feel those emotions too. These stances can be used to calm a stressed listener, to charge up an audience, or to make another person comfortable during a conversation.

The first Satir stance is that of the *placater,* which is used to keep the person you're speaking to from becoming angry. Then there is the *blamer,* which we use to compensate for our own feelings of weakness by shifting responsibility onto someone else. The *distracter* stance is used to change the subject of a conversation. It is rooted in the speaker's need to believe that if he or she ignores a problem, it will disappear. There is also the *computer* stance, characterized by a speaker's effort to dissociate themselves from the intense emotions of a conversation by using intellectual terms to analyze the situation. Last but not least is the *leveler,* a stance from which a speaker reveals the truth about his or her current situation and emotions.

Each Satir stance can be used to change one or more of the other stances. For example, the placater stance helps to shift the blamer's focus from his own point of view to yours. Conversely, the blamer stance can be used to balance the placater's perspective of you, herself, and the situation. Both the placating and blaming stances will cause a computer to shift into a placater or blamer stance himself, and the computer can be used to shift the stance of a distracter.

Once you have used one stance to change the stance of another, you can calibrate your behavior to balance theirs. You can create rapport with a leveler by assuming a leveler stance yourself, but when it comes to all the other stances, mirroring them will produce bad results. A conversation between two blamers, for example, will quickly turn into a heated argument. On the other hand, two computers will bore each other and two placaters will allow one another to wallow unproductively in their misery, never reaching a solution to their problem. And, as you may have already concluded, a conversation between two distracters would border on utter nonsense.

The Satir stances are most effective when used together. In switching from one to the other, a public speaker creates and manipulates an emotional pace, guiding the reactions of his audience in order to create a feeling of good rapport, trust, and ultimately agreement with or belief in the speaker's assertions. Masterful use of the Satir stances can build a motivational speaker's audience, get a politician elected to office, or help a teacher obtain and maintain the attention and respect of her students.

The following are detailed descriptions of each Satir stance. Practice them until they begin to flow naturally into your everyday conversations. In mastering these non-verbal communication techniques, you will improve your relationships with friends, family, and co-workers, and you will increase your own productivity as well as that of the people you work with on a regular basis.

The Placater: Stand with your feet shoulder width apart, body directly facing your listeners. Keep your hips level and turn your palms upward in supplication. Position your head vertically or tilt it very slightly while raising the eyebrows in a questioning or even a pleading manner.

The Blamer: Face your body directly toward your listener and lean forward slightly while lowering both your head and eyebrows just a bit. To create an attack effect, point one index finger directly at the audience, and to warn of an impending attack, point it at the ceiling.

The Computer: To give the impression of consideration or evaluation, square your torso with your audience and lean back slightly on one foot. Rest one forearm across your chest and rest the elbow of the other arm on it, extending the hand upward to support the chin. Keep your head level and furrow your brow slightly as if thinking.

The Distracter: Raise one eyebrow and smile wryly while shifting the body and limbs into varying positions in order to repeatedly change your angle to your audience.

The Leveler: To portray honesty and credibility, stand with your feet shoulder width apart, facing your body directly toward your audience and keeping your hips, shoulders, and head level. Relax your face and eyebrows. Bring your hands up, palms facing down, and spread them slightly wider than your shoulders as if you are leaning on a table.

Together, the Satir stances form a solid foundation for the effective use of non-verbal communication. There are other techniques that can be layered over them in order to add emphasis to your speech and further impact your listeners. These techniques essentially turn your body into an amplifier for verbal expression. Most people already use these amplifiers naturally and unconsciously, but in applying them with awareness, you heighten the emotions of your audience, significantly increasing their level of engagement. Emphasis techniques can be applied to the voice as well as the body, but a mismatch in the two signals can result in mixed messages that will look to your audience like sarcasm or dishonesty, neither of which bolster your credibility. For this reason, it is recommended that you practice one until it comes naturally to you *and then* layer the other on top of it.

There are two types of emphasis techniques: *exaggerated* and *subtle.* The key to making the most of them is to synchronize all of your tools for non-verbal communication. These tools, as previously discussed, include body positioning, movement, eye contact, and tone of voice among other things. These elements must work in concert, each one sending the same message, in order to project a solid, believable message rather than a cacophony of confusion.

Exaggerated emphasis is used to produce the energy needed to drive home a point. The goal is to overpower your opponent or audience with sheer force of passion. Exaggerated emphasis techniques are usually aggressive in nature. They include wide, sweeping gestures, vigorous nodding or shaking of the head, and dramatic facial expressions. You might pound a fist on the podium or stomp your foot in time with your most important points. Your gestures and movements are bigger and faster, and they make use of the entire stage. You might also alternate between movement and stillness to create a dynamic contrast that will engage your listeners.

When overused or applied at the wrong moment, emphasis techniques can intimidate your audience and make them feel they are being coerced. They may then become suspicious of your motives, at which point you've destroyed your chances at winning them over. Depending on your audience, you may want to use less aggressive exaggerated emphasis techniques. These include moving toward your audience as you make important points, reaching out to them, simulating embraces, and gazing directly at your listeners without blinking. Repetitive movements—especially rhythmic ones—create a hypnotic effect that essentially beats your points into the minds of your listeners.

Exaggerated emphasis, whether aggressive or not, is best used with large audiences in large, open spaces or auditoriums. In a one-on-one situation, or with a small group, subtle emphasis techniques will be much more effective. These techniques work best when you are relaxed, and it helps to approach your audience as though they are delicate and fragile.

The first element for subtle emphasis is small movements. Things like finger and wrist gestures work well, as do barely perceptible changes in facial expression and small tilts of the head. Shape is another important element of subtle emphasis. Cup your palm as if you're holding something fragile or point your feet in a certain direction. Your third element is light contact. Glance at your listeners briefly like you're checking to see if they're paying attention, step or lean toward them, or nod in agreement.

When layered over a solid understanding and mastery of the Satir stances, both exaggerated and subtle emphasis will add power to your speech and engage your audience. Practice all these techniques until they are second nature and learn to gauge your audience in order to choose the best method or combination of methods. In doing so, you prepare yourself to persuade, gain trust, and create positive relationships in any situation.

Chapter 5: Tips & Troubleshooting

An understanding of body language can turn almost any difficult situation into a productive one. This alone makes it indispensable. But there is another application for this knowledge which makes it invaluable: it can be used as a lie detector. If a person's words or behavior seem suspicious, analyze the five basic components of their body language. Are they facing you, or is their body turned away? Are they making eye contact, or are their eyes moving rapidly about, looking at everything but you? Look for redness in the face or neck, an increase in perspiration or breathing rate, fingers or hands over the mouth, or a rise in vocal pitch. These are all words in the body language vocabulary of lies, and in learning to spot them, you increase your personal safety and security and prepare yourself to make the best decisions in any situation.

While serving as your own lie detector seems convenient, it is wise to use this ability very carefully. This is the area in which most people make interpretation mistakes. It is important to refrain from making assumptions and jumping to conclusions. Body language varies slightly from one person to another, just as the English accent differs from one country to another. It varies due to cultural differences, past experiences, and a host of other factors, and we don't always have time to get to know a person well enough to accurately interpret their dialect of non-verbal communication. One person's nervousness might resemble another person's untruthfulness. One person's confusion might resemble another person's defensiveness. If you notice any of the above behaviors, invite the person who is exhibiting them to share their thoughts and feelings. This will enable you to respond in the most productive way possible.

Keep in mind that body language is not x-ray vision. It does not reveal a person's inner workings immediately and in detail. But when combined with patience and persistence, it will lead you to a better understanding of almost anyone you may encounter, and it will allow you to take charge in nearly every type of situation.

Monitoring and refining your own body language at all times is also challenging. In order to do so, you would have to maintain a constant awareness of each of the hundreds of muscles in your body and manage them to ensure that they would respond only to your conscious instructions and not to emotional signals from your subconscious. At the same time, you would have to decipher non-verbal communications from others *and* perform whatever tasks are required to achieve your current goal. The face alone is comprised of 90 muscles that constantly broadcast emotions, and it will be the focal point for your audience in every situation. In reality, it would be virtually impossible to control *all* of your non-verbal signals, and in trying too hard to do so, you send mixed messages that your audience will perceive either consciously or subconsciously. This makes your listeners uncomfortable, arousing their suspicion and corroding their trust in you.

At this point, you may be questioning the value of studying body language, but don't be discouraged. Complete control is not necessary. An understanding of body language will enhance the effectiveness of your communication abilities as long as you simply remain aware of it and use it in careful, subtle ways that feel natural to you. Start small. Pay attention to your own behaviors, and if you notice yourself crossing your arms or bouncing your foot up and down during a conversation, ask yourself why. This will lead you to a better understanding of your relationship with your environment, making you more comfortable and increasing your self-confidence.

It's also important not to allow the potential for misinterpretation deter you from taking advantage of non-verbal communication. Instead, practice deciphering the non-verbal signals of others. There are various ways you can hone your ability to read physical signs and signals. The best method is observation, or *people watching*. Observe people in coffee shops, on the subway, and when you walk down the street. Mute your television and try to guess the plot of a sitcom based on the gestures of the characters. You will not always be able to verify whether or not your assumptions are correct, but observation is valuable in that it trains you to *pay attention* to body language. This is the first step toward correctly interpreting the non-verbal communications of others, and to effectively communicating your own thoughts and feelings through body language.

Like any other tool, an understanding of the use and interpretation of body language can be employed with good or bad intentions. Using body language to project confidence is good for both you and your listeners in a variety of situations. But using it to persuade someone to do something that is not in their nature or best interests is manipulative at best. It is important to keep in mind that no one can control every aspect of their body language at all times, and that your listener may be as adept as you in the art of interpreting physical signals. There is always a chance that he or she will discover your negative intentions through signals you don't know you're sending, and that the discrepancy between what you're trying to project and what may be slipping through the cracks will damage your credibility and your reputation. Always be careful to gauge your situation, read your audience, and apply body language in the most positive way possible.

The best way to ensure that you are using body language to your advantage is to make sure that your subconscious mind is in agreement with your conscious mind. If your daily life is one long string of uncomfortable situations in which you find yourself contradicting your real feelings with your body language, perhaps you need to rethink your daily life. Reconsider your goals, your beliefs, and your values. Ask yourself if they really belong to you. Are you trying to get a promotion because your wife is pressuring you to being home a bigger paycheck, or do you *really want* the job? Are you still attending that Catholic church because your mother wants you too, or does that particular spirituality really satisfy you? Do you really want a huge house and an expensive car, or would you rather sell all your possessions and start backpacking across China? Once you align your outer life with your inner desires, your conscious mind ceases to be in conflict with your subconscious mind. Your body language begins to reflect your true emotions, at which point, you will no longer need to force your non-verbal behaviors to exude confidence because it will come naturally.

Chapter 6: The Benefits of Understanding Body Language

Don't judge a book by its cover. That's the common wisdom. But what if you could? Wouldn't it make life a lot easier? In a way, reading and interpreting body language equals just that. But it isn't the same as pinning a stranger to a stereotype based on the clothes they're wearing. It allows you to figure out who the *individual* is based on *their own* style of non-verbal communication.

There are so many situations in which this ability is invaluable. Are you the human resources manager at your business? If you could hear what an interviewee *wasn't* telling you, hiring the right person for the job would be much easier. Less time and money would be wasted in training the kinds of people who interview well and then make a 180-degree about face once they're hired. All the qualities an interviewer looks for can be faked, and according to studies, they often are. There is little connection between the charismatic, self-promotional interview personality and actual skill level and workplace behavior. An understanding of body language enables you to see past the charismatic interview personality and determine your interviewee's real potential in relation to the job you're offering.

The only thing more challenging than choosing great employees is choosing your life partner. There are tons of fish in the sea. One of them has got to be the right person for you, but you've only got so much time to fish. It would be great if we didn't have to spend so much of our precious time wondering how others felt about us. And although such relationships teach us a lot of valuable lessons, it would also be nice to spend less time getting involved with people who seem perfect for us at first only to find out after three months that we aren't compatible with them at all.

The non-verbal signals used in flirting are hard-wired into us. We've been using and refining them since human life first began. But while we can all tell if someone is interested in us, it would be even better if we could tell *how* they are interested in us. Is this man after a one-night stand, or is he my future husband and soul mate? Maybe he just wants to be friends. Real flirting involves distinctive signals. For example, men and women both tend to attract their person of interest with big smiles. During conversation, women use sing-song vocal tones while men drop their vocal tones into a lower register. As mutual interest increases, the two begin to mimic one another's posture and gestures. An ability to read body language will help you to more accurately decipher the other person's intentions and desires.

Sometimes, even when that dream job or that potential soul mate are not at stake, an encounter with another person can be surprisingly rattling. You walk away from your first meeting with a complete stranger marveling uncomfortably at what a disaster it was and wondering how it could have gone so badly. Maybe it started to go downhill when you began to sense the other person's disinterest in your attempts at friendly small-talk. Maybe it spiraled into the abyss when you realized you were never going to get a single word in. Perhaps it all went bad when the other person misinterpreted a bit of sarcasm and became deeply offended.

Shyness, introversion, anxiety, autism, and a host of other attributes contribute to conversations like these. And sometimes two personalities just don't mix. In developing your ability to read the body language of others and refine your own non-verbal communications, you learn to differentiate between less socially adept personalities and people who are actually trying to offend. You also develop an ability to make others more comfortable around you. It becomes much easier to interact with those whose conversational styles are different from yours, and misinterpretations occur less frequently.

In addition to improving your interactions with well-meaning but socially awkward individuals, an understanding of body language will enhance your ability to discern the malicious intentions of actual manipulators.

Studies have consistently shown that confidence and charisma change minds and amass devoted followers. Most of us look at extreme examples of this—like the charismatic televangelist who spends the money of his millions of devotees on private planes and limousines—and we think to ourselves, *I would have seen right through that.* But would we? Does confidence really equal power?

The answer is yes. United States culture is especially supportive of this idea. The problem lies in the fact that because confidence is exhibited via clusters of non-verbal signals, it can be faked. Your ability to read body language will empower you to see through the facades of "powerful" people with bad intentions. And there is, of course, a more positive side to this coin. Because a change in physical posture can change mental processes, using confident signals yourself will enable you to inspire and motivate others in situations where you must take the lead. Just be careful not to overdo it. Reveling too much in your own power can injure your ability to see situations from other points of view, which will ultimately lead to the deterioration of relationships of all types.

Understanding non-verbal communication will lead to improvement in all areas of your life. It will improve your relationships and contribute to your success in the workplace. When used wisely, it will help you achieve your grandest dreams.

Conclusion

An understanding of body language is essential to effective communication. Our gestures, eye movements, and tone of voice say everything that our words do not. In aligning our non-verbal signals with our words, we send clearer, stronger messages and make longer-lasting impressions. We enable ourselves to convey our true feelings and to accurately interpret the true thoughts and emotions of others. In doing so, we gain the confidence, trust, and support of others and make it easier to accomplish our goals.

While learning to use and interpret single acts of non-verbal communication is useful, learning to decipher clusters of signals is best. Being aware of contradictions between the various actions within another person's cluster of signals can help us determine whether or not they are being genuine. Just remember to take context into consideration when interpreting these discrepancies, as a person may not necessarily be reacting to their present situation.

It is also advantageous to look out for micro-expressions and to maintain an awareness of socially accepted comfort zones while speaking with others. Remember that body language varies based on one's personality, life experience, and culture, and try to adjust your non-verbal communications accordingly in order to make the person you're talking with more comfortable.

The ability to read the body language of another person or a group of people allows us to get and maintain attention and interest, and it helps us to persuade people to support our efforts. The skill of body language interpretation also helps us more accurately determine how others feel about us, which helps us to avoid relationships that are bound to go bad eventually. Just remember to consider the context of another's actions in order to ensure that they are interested in the same type of relationship that interests you.

Refining your own body language will help you develop confidence, which will lead to an increase in power and influence. You can do this by learning the Satir stances, integrating them into your non-verbal vocabulary, and layering both exaggerated and subtle emphasis techniques on top of them. In order to use these technique effectively, you must learn to gauge your audience and determine which approach will work best given your intentions and your situation.

Do not be discouraged if you cannot immediately interpret everyone's body language with unfaltering accuracy, or if you continue to make mistakes with your own non-verbal signals. Mastery of non-verbal communication takes time and practice. Just remember to avoid jumping to conclusions too quickly. Also, remember to use body language carefully. There is a big difference between influence and manipulation, and the latter often backfires on its user. Make sure to always employ your new-found insights and abilities with your best interests and the best interests of others in mind, because positive intentions yield positive results.

Keep in mind that it is near impossible to control all of your non-verbal signals all the time, and that trying too hard to do so can elicit suspicion from your audience and lead to a decrease in trust. If you find that you must constantly adjust your non-verbal signals in order to cover up your true feelings, it is time to rethink your intentions. In making sure that your conscious desires match your subconscious desires, you avoid sending mixed messages and increase both your own confidence and the level of confidence others have in you.

Non-verbal communication is just as important as verbal expression, if not more so. It allows us to project our true feelings and detect the true feelings of others. It improves our relationships and our leadership skills and gives us the confidence to persuade and influence. Now is the time to start learning to read and refine body language. In doing so, you increase your chances at success in every area of your life.

www.ingramcontent.com/pod-product-compliance
Lightning Source LLC
Chambersburg PA
CBHW070821290526
45795CB00002B/804